# Ireland:

## *The True and Surprising Stories of Irish History*

From Hero To Zero

© Copyright 2017 by From Hero To Zero- All rights reserved.

The follow eBook is reproduced below with the goal of providing information that is as accurate and reliable as possible. Regardless, purchasing this eBook can be seen as consent to the fact that both the publisher and the author of this book are in no way experts on the topics discussed within and that any recommendations or suggestions that are made herein are for entertainment purposes only. Professionals should be consulted as needed prior to undertaking any of the action endorsed herein.

This declaration is deemed fair and valid by both the American Bar Association and the Committee of Publishers Association and is legally binding throughout the United States.

Furthermore, the transmission, duplication or reproduction of any of the following work including specific information will be considered an illegal act irrespective of if it is done electronically or in print. This extends to creating a secondary or tertiary copy of the work or a recorded copy and is only allowed with express written consent from the Publisher. All additional right reserved.

The information in the following pages is broadly considered to be a truthful and accurate account of facts and as such any inattention, use or misuse of the information in question by the reader will render any resulting actions solely under their purview. There are no scenarios in which the publisher or the original author of this work can be in any fashion deemed liable for any hardship or damages that may befall them after undertaking information described herein.

Additionally, the information in the following pages is intended only for informational purposes and should thus be thought of as universal. As befitting its nature, it is presented without assurance regarding its prolonged validity or interim quality. Trademarks that are mentioned are done without written consent and can in no way be considered an endorsement from the trademark holder.

# Table of Contents

About The Book ............................................................................................. 5
Introduction ................................................................................................... 6
Chapter One: Ireland .................................................................................... 7
Chapter Two: Ireland Before It was Ireland ................................................ 9
   *Early Medieval Times* ............................................................................ *12*
**Chapter Three: Irish Economy** ................................................................ **15**
   *Tourism* .................................................................................................. *15*
   *Energy* .................................................................................................... *16*
**Chapter Four: The Black Death** .............................................................. **18**
   *Entryway* ............................................................................................... *18*
   *Mortality unheard of* ........................................................................... *19*
   *Spreading rapidly* ................................................................................. *21*
**Chapter Five: Viking Ireland** ................................................................... **22**
   *Arriving in Ireland* ................................................................................ *22*
   *Settlement in Ireland* ........................................................................... *22*
   *Attacks on the towns of Ireland* .......................................................... *23*
   *Irish monasteries* .................................................................................. *24*
   *The Irish rebel* ...................................................................................... *24*
   *No victory in sight* ................................................................................ *25*
**Chapter Six: St. Patrick** ........................................................................... **27**
   *Captured by the Irish* ........................................................................... *27*
   *Visions* .................................................................................................... *28*
   *Crosses and bonfires* ............................................................................ *29*
   *Legends of St. Patrick* .......................................................................... *30*
   *The shamrock* ....................................................................................... *30*
   *Banishing the snakes* ........................................................................... *31*
   *Patricks' walking stick* .......................................................................... *31*
   *The ancient ancestors and Patrick speak* ........................................... *31*
   *Saint Patrick's Cross* ............................................................................. *32*
   *Saint Patrick's Bell* ................................................................................ *33*
   *Places that are associated with St. Patrick* ........................................ *33*
   *Places named after Patrick* .................................................................. *34*
   *St. Patrick's Day* .................................................................................... *35*
   *Fun facts* ................................................................................................ *35*

    Snakes in Ireland ............................................................................................. 35
    Partying ............................................................................................................ 36
    Green ................................................................................................................ 36
    Shamrocks ........................................................................................................ 36
    Leprechauns ..................................................................................................... 37
    Corned beef and cabbage ............................................................................... 37
**Chapter Seven: The Irish Rebellion ............................................................... 38**
    *Background information .................................................................................. 38*
    *Society of United Irishmen .............................................................................. 39*
    *1796 .................................................................................................................. 40*
    *Counterinsurgency and repression ................................................................. 40*
    *Rebellion ........................................................................................................... 42*
    *Aftermath ......................................................................................................... 43*
**Chapter Eight: The Nine Years' War ............................................................... 44**
    *Causes ............................................................................................................... 44*
    *The crown and Ulster ....................................................................................... 45*
    *War .................................................................................................................... 45*
    *An Irish victory ................................................................................................. 46*
    *The rebellion ends in Munster ........................................................................ 47*
    *End of the war ................................................................................................. 48*
**Chapter Nine: Bloody Sunday ........................................................................ 49**
    *Bloody Sunday morning ................................................................................... 50*
    *Bloody Sunday afternoon ................................................................................ 51*
    *Bloody Sunday night ........................................................................................ 53*
    *Misconceptions ................................................................................................ 53*
**Chapter Ten: The Partition of Ireland ............................................................ 54**
    *Background ....................................................................................................... 55*
    *Ireland act ........................................................................................................ 55*
    *Anglo-Irish treaty ............................................................................................. 56*
    *Northern Ireland .............................................................................................. 56*
**Chapter Eleven: The IRA (Irish Republican Army) ......................................... 58**
**Chapter Twelve: Ireland Today ...................................................................... 61**
    *Irish flags .......................................................................................................... 62*
**Chapter Thirteen: Interesting Facts about Ireland ........................................ 64**
**Conclusion ..................................................................................................... 66**
**Free Kindle Books ......................................................................................... 67**

# About The Book

Ireland has a very rich and intense history, and the more that you know about it, the more you are going to fall in love with the emerald isle.

The purpose of this book is to give you some knowledge that you may not have regarding Ireland and its history. You may, of course, know of some of the events that happened in Ireland, but you may not know all of the history that is behind those events. Not only that, but you may have some misinformation about the history of Ireland and here is where it is going to be straightened out!

So, I hope you enjoy reading this book as much as I enjoyed writing it!

# Introduction

Congratulations on downloading *Ireland* and thank you for doing so.

The following chapters will discuss the history of Ireland and some of the more surprising facts that you may not know about the Emerald Isle. There is a rich history of Ireland that many people do not know about and even if they do know, they do not know everything.

In this book, you are going to learn the true history of some of the stories that you have heard about Ireland! There are going to be some things that you may have heard before about the history of Ireland – however, what you have heard before may end up only being a legend! This book covers the remarkable story of this beautiful region.

There are plenty of books on this subject on the market, thanks again for choosing this one! Every effort was made to ensure it is full of as much useful information as possible, please enjoy!

# Chapter One: Ireland

While the rest of the world says Ireland, in Irish it is pronounced Eire and in Ulster Scots, it is pronounced Airlann. This island is located in the North Atlantic Ocean and has a straight path to Great Britain by way of the North Channel, St. George's channel, and the Irish sea.

This island is one of the two largest islands that are a part of the British Isles and it is the third largest island in Europe. However, compared to the rest of the world, it is only the twentieth largest island.

Interestingly enough, Ireland is separated politically into the Republic of Ireland, which is what is officially known as Ireland, and Northern Ireland. The Republic of Ireland covers around five-sixths of the island. In the meantime, Northern Ireland is under the control of the United Kingdom and is the northeast part of the island. Back in 2011, the population of Ireland made it the second most populated island in Europe. Out of the entire population of Ireland as a whole, only 1.8 million are living in Northern Ireland while the remaining 4.6 million are living in the Republic of Ireland.

Most of Ireland is mountains along with several rivers that wind their way through it. The whole of Ireland is absolutely covered with lush vegetation thanks to the mild temperature climate that they experience.

Until the Middle Ages, there were thick woodlands that covered a great majority of the island. However, in 2013, only about eleven percent of woods covered the Irish mainland.
Out of all the mammals that were in Ireland, at least twenty-six

are native to Ireland and still alive. But, because of the climate being an oceanic one, the winters of the regions rife with wildlife are not nearly as cold as some parts of the state experience due largely to where they are located. The summers are also cooler but the only downside is that there are clouds that cover the island almost constantly and rainfall is very abundant.

The settlement of Ireland can be dated back to 10,500 BC, which is about the time period that the first evidence of human involvement crops up. In the first century, the pagan Gaelic Ireland first developed as a society before being Christianized in the fifth century. During the twelfth century the Normans invaded Ireland and England claimed Ireland in the name of their kingdom.

Surprisingly enough, England did not rule over all of Ireland until around the sixteenth and maybe even the seventeenth centuries during the Tudor conquests. By 1690, there was a system put in place by the English, who were Protestant, that made it to where the Catholics were at a disadvantage, which made it so that the Protestants ruled over Ireland until sometime around the eighteenth century.

The Acts of Union occurred in 1801 and made Ireland part of the United Kingdom once and for all. There was a war that broke out around the beginning of the twentieth century for Ireland to have its independence, and this is when the island was split in half and the Irish Free State was created. During the '60s all the way to the '90s, there was a lot of civil unrest that occurred in the Northern part of Ireland. Thankfully a political agreement was reached in 1998. However, in '73 the European Economic Community was joined by the Republic of Ireland, which caused Northern Ireland and the United Kingdom to follow.

# Chapter Two: Ireland Before It was Ireland

Sometime around 9000 years ago, it was the last of the glacial period and much of Ireland was covered in ice. The sea levels were lowered in Ireland and sometime around 12,000 BC, the sea levels rose and the ice melted causing Ireland to separate from Great Britain and become its own island.

You can look back to 10,500 BC and see that there was indeed a human presence in Ireland which caused the theory of the Mesolithic people to being the first people on the island of Ireland, having come over from Britain sometime between 8000 and 7000 BC.

In around 4500 BC the Neolithic settlers first began to populate Ireland. It was these settlers that began to introduce cereal cultivars. They also would be the ones to develop some stone monuments. Agriculture began to grow more advanced and thus the Ceide Fields were developed, which is now in the region known as Tyrawley.

The Ceide Fields, if you're wondering, is a large field system that one can see for themselves in Ireland today, and it is considered to be one of the oldest found in the world. The field system has different divisions that have been separated by a wall. It is believed that these fields are from between 3500 and 3000 BC. The two main crops that were grown there was wheat and barley which was imported from the peninsula of Iberian.

During the Bronze Age, the technology that was developing

rapidly continued to change everyone's lives, and it was during this period of time where things like the weaving of textiles, metalworking, the wheel, and even the brewing of alcohol came into play thanks to all of the new tools and weapons that were produced.

Not only were weapons and tools created, but jewelry was created too. The jewelry that was created was made with gold for things such as torcs and brooches.

Researchers have stated that in the late Bronze Age, Ireland became part of a major trading network that was known as the Atlantic Bronze age and it was here that the Celtic languages were developed and then brought back to Ireland. However, the traditional views that are seen on Ireland contradict this because people believe that the origin of the Celtic language came from the Hallstatt culture.

Moving on to the Iron Age, the Celtic language and their culture began to emerge in Ireland. For over a century researchers have been going back and forth on when Ireland first became Celtic and how this change occurred. One of the themes that continues to come up is that the Celts migrated to Ireland. However, as time rolls on and there are more studies done both linguistically and archaeologically, more thoughts have been coming up.

One theory that does not seem to be argued with is that the Ogham script, the culture, and the Celtic language are from the Celts that came over to Ireland from Europe in order to invade. The theory comes from the Lebor Gabala Erenn which is one of the pseudo-histories that come from the medieval Christians about the history of Ireland and how the Celtic culture got there.

Things like Celtic bronze torcs, shields, spears and many other possessions have been found which leads most historians to believe that the Celts invaded Ireland at least four times. The Priteni are believed to be the first ones who invaded the island which was followed by the Belgae. From there the Laighin tribe invaded and then the last to invade were the Milesians.

Whenever the second wave of the Euerni came to Ireland, they began to arrive in the sixth century. It is said that they gave their name to the island.

Some of the more recent theories that have been found to be supported amongst many archaeologists are that the Celtic culture and their language come from a diffusion of different cultures. The theory goes on to say that Celticisation in Ireland was the culmination of a process of different interactions which occurred on a social and economic standpoint between Britain, Ireland, and other parts of the Continental Europe.

There is no evidence for the immigration of the Celts, but it is somehow accepted that these movements were notoriously hard to identify. It is more likely that the Celts moved into Ireland in smaller batches and it was just enough traffic to be considered a migration. The linguists studying the Celtic language, however, are not as easily convinced that this method is the primary method that would cause the absorption of the language like was seen on the island.

Investigations into different lineages that are in the area where it is believed that the Celtic migrations took place shows that there are no major differences to be found in the mitochondrial DNA between those that lived in Ireland and those who lived in larger areas of continental Europe. The only differences that could be found were in some of the patterns that are located on the Y chromosome.

However, when you look at recent studies that have been done, those who speak Celtic today are considered to be European "Atlantic Celts" that have an ancestry that is shared by a great majority of the Atlantic zone which spreads from northern Iberia to the western parts of Scandinavia rather than staying in central Europe.

## Early Medieval Times

Some of the earliest written records can be found were penned by Greco-Roman archaeologists. In Almagest, written by Ptolemy, there is much written about Ireland as "the smaller island of Britain" and how much smaller it is than the larger island of Great Britain.

In his later works, he writes about Ireland as Iouernia while Great Britain was referred to as Albion. The new names were probably chosen because of the names that were associated with the islands at the time. However, the names that he gave to the islands in his early works were probably given out because of the contact that he had made with the people that resided there.

Ireland was a patchwork of many kingdoms that were fighting, however, when the seventh century came around, there was a concept introduced for national kingship which eventually evolved into the concept of a high king of Ireland.

Literature from medieval Ireland shows that there was a

sequence that was nearly unbroken about the high kings and it dated back thousands of years. However, historians now days think that this as a scheme that was created in the eighth century so that they could try and justify how powerful some of the political groups had gotten so that they could try and project the origins of their rule from the remote past.

Any kingdom that was in Ireland at the time had their own kings and they all fell under the high king. This high king was the one who ruled over all of the provincial kings as well as the kingdom of Meath which was the ceremonial capital located at the Hill of Tara. This whole concept became a reality during the Viking age and it was not consistently used. Ireland did have a unifying rule of law though and this is one of the earliest written judicial systems where the Brehon Laws were administered by jurists called brehons.

There are Chronicles of Ireland that were recorded sometime in 431 around the time of Bishop Palladius arriving in Ireland after Pope Celestine the first had sent him there to preach to those living in Ireland that believed in Christianity already. This bishop is said to have arrived just a year before Patrick did when he went to minister to those who did not believe. Sadly, there is still some debate on Palladius and Patrick and when they were in Ireland.

Some older druid traditions collapsed when Christianity was brought to Ireland. The Christian scholars in Ireland were excellent in studying Latin and Greek along with studying and learning about the new Christian technology that had been brought to the island.

The culture that came after the Christianisation of Ireland caused the learning of Greek and Latin to be preserved in the culture of Ireland whenever the Early Middle Ages came about all the way up to the fall of the Western Roman Empire.

Things such as manuscript illumination, metalworking and even the creation of sculptures continued to advance in Ireland. Things such as the Book of Kells, stone crosses that were hand carved, and ornate jewelry were produced, some of which are still being produced on the island to this very day.

A mission was founded by Saint Columba to spread the Celtic Christianity to Scotland, the Frankish Empire, and England, sometime after the fall of Rome. Well into the late Middle Ages, centers for learning and monasteries were being built and causing a major influence in Europe.

# Chapter Three: Irish Economy

There may be two different jurisdictions, but that simply means that there are two currencies being used. This caused a growth in the commercial activity that Ireland experienced to be carried out on an all-Ireland basis. This caused two jurisdictions to have a membership that was shared by the European Union. Members are from different businesses in the community as well as those that made policies so that there was a full coverage of those who made up the Irish economy so that Ireland could take advantage of the competitive boost and economies of scale.

In Ireland, there are two regions that consist of several cities located in Ireland.

1. Cork-Limerick-Galway corridor
2. Dublin-Belfast corridor

## Tourism

On the island of Ireland, there are three world heritage sites. These three sites are:

1. Giant's Causeway
2. Brun a Boinne
3. Skellig Michael

There are plenty of other places that may become part of the list however they are not officially part of the tourism scene in Ireland.

Many places that are often visited by those who come to visit Ireland are the Cliffs of Moher, Bunratty Castle, Holy Cross Abbey, Rock of Cashel, and the Blarney Castle. Some of the more monastic sites would include the national monuments that are located in the Republic of Ireland, the Glendalough and the Clonmacnoise.

Historically, the most tourists can be found in Dublin because of everything that it has to offer for a tourist.

Off the coast, there is the Achill island which is one of the largest islands that is a part of Ireland. The tourists that are looking to surf usually go to this island and visit the homes that were built during the seventeenth, eighteenth, and nineteenth century in neo-Gothic styles. A few of these homes are actually hotels where the tourists can stay so they do not have to go back to the main island.

# Energy

Peat is one of the main sources of energy in Ireland. This is a form of biomass energy that is a great source of heat and it is still used in the more rural areas. But, because of how important the peatlands are to the economy in storing carbon and how rare they are, the EU is trying to protect these lands. Therefore, if the peat is dug up, there is a heavy fine that is laid on Ireland for doing so.

In the Irish cities, heat is normally given out by heating oils however there are some suppliers in the cities that are trying to give out smokeless fuel know as sods of turf.

There are some areas of the island that work on a single market when it comes to the electricity. For a great majority of their existence, the electric networks found in the Republic of Ireland and Northern Ireland were separated from each other due to the partition. But, because of the changes that occurred over the recent years, they are not connected as well as being connected to the mainland Europe.

In Northern Ireland there are some issues with companies not giving enough power to the NIE (Northern Ireland Electricity), and the ESB in the Republic of Ireland has not modernized their power stations. The combination of these two factors leaves the availability around sixty-six percent which is one of the worst to be located in Europe.

Transmission lines from EirGrid are being built so that they can stretch between Great Britain and Ireland giving 500 megawatts of electricity, which will cover about ten percent of the demand that is in Ireland.

# Chapter Four: The Black Death

The Black Death and the effect that it had on Ireland are hard to talk about because of how little is actually recorded about them. Not only that, but the economy was not doing that well before the plague ever made its way to Ireland in 1348, making it hard to know the economic impact either. Despite all of the setbacks, there is just enough information that has been found to show how the Black Death affected Ireland and how the outbreaks continued to leave a lasting effect on the Emerald Isle.

## Entryway

How the plague affected everything it touched was not the same in each place. The Anglo-Irish people were affected in a way that was more radical than those who were part of Gaelic Ireland.

The first outbreak of Black Death was at the ports where rats - who were infected because of the fleas they'd picked up - came in off the holds of the ships that they stowed away in. If they were not in the holds then they were in the merchandise that was coming onto the island.

Friar John Clyn suggested that the plague first appeared in Dalkey and even Howth before it made its way inland towards Dublin which happened towards the end of July and even early August. There was a very short period of time that fell between when the plague was first showing in Bristol as well as in

Ireland which would ultimately suggest that the plague was brought straight to Ireland from the Bordeaux region.

The paths of transmission for the rest of the country were through routes that occurred overland between the various towns, markets, and ports. Anywhere that the merchandise went that came off the boats with infected rats soon found that they were infected as well.

Areas that were not yet touched by the plague were being invaded by an airborne form that occurred more heavily during the winter months which showed that there was a higher transmission of the plague between humans which caused it to spread quicker and thus lead to a higher death rate.

# Mortality unheard of

Between August and December, the plague took over Dublin which also brought in the terror that people began to feel as it spread through the other parts of the country. Friar Clyn wrote, "From very fear and horror, men were seldom brave enough to perform the works of piety and mercy, such as visiting the sick and burying the dead."

There were sermons delivered that hinted at those who survived being the ones who took over property that was now owned by women who had been widowed and minors. There were others who responded to the epidemic by praying or going on what is known as a pilgrimage. The public functions that had been planned were canceled because of the outbreak as a precaution to be able to try and stop it from spreading.

Sometime during 1350, the pestilence was still contagious and anyone that touched someone that was sick or someone that had died was going to ultimately become infected with the plague and end up dying.

Clyn also wrote: "There was hardly a house in which one only had died, but as a rule, man and wife with their children and all the family went the common way of death."

The friars and abbeys were the ones that ended up getting hit the hardest because they were the ones who were administering last rights to those who were dying. Yet, the plague continued to spread throughout the towns and villages leaving almost no one unaffected.

The plague came in two different strains, pneumonic and bubonic all of which had similar symptoms but were different in ways as well. The bubonic strains were those that were transmitted from flea bites and brought on pustules that appeared on one's groin or under their armpits. Along with that, the victims also spit up blood and had headaches that were distinguished from the pneumonic form of the plague.

The first direct contact transmission most likely occurred in Dublin before the outbreak overtook Ireland. Even as it moved through the first stages it probably began to be transmitted in other ways that were not pneumonic as it moved away from the larger towns and onto the areas that had fewer people living together. As it went through the countryside, it was probably mostly transmitted by the rats and fleas which was going to be determined by how large the population of rats was which then depended on how many humans were living together and how much trade was done in that area.

# Spreading rapidly

Before 1348 could come to a close, Louth was overtaken by the plague and it has reached as far as Kilkenny by Christmas of that year. Because of how long it took for the plague to reach these cities suggests that it did not go overland, but along the rivers instead. Friar Clyn writes that there were at least eight friars that were dead in a single day alone and that the pestilence was still rife between December and March of the next year.

However, because of how contagious the plague was, it was not going to be stopped and it was going to spread through the community of Clyn's Franciscan and to the rest of the inhabitants of the town.

# Chapter Five: Viking Ireland

Whenever Vikings came to Ireland, they were the first people to come to the island in great masses since the Celts that first arrived there during the Iron age. It was for about eight centuries that Ireland enjoyed peace from any attacks that came externally unlike Britain who was constantly under attack from the Romans and the Germanic people.

## Arriving in Ireland

The first round of Vikings to land on the shores of Ireland hailed from Scandinavia and they were not trying to wage war, rather find some new lands where they could begin to create settlements.

But, in 795 AD, the first attacks came from the Vikings thanks to Irish monks that were in the Annals of Ulster.

The Viking attacks continued for about forty more years even though they were happening at a rate of one or two attacks a year. Each attack that came from the Vikings was resisted by the natives of Ireland and sometime in 811, the Vikings were slaughtered as they tried to raid Ulster. Sometime in 823, the Vikings returned once more and attacked Bangor, and other similar attacks continued in the year that followed.

## Settlement in Ireland

The first Vikings that came to Ireland were unsure of what lay inland on the island so they stayed about twenty miles from the coast and kept their attacks along the coast sticking to the monasteries that they came across. In the first winter, settlements that were more permanent were made at Lough Neagh.

The year that followed the first winter that the Vikings spent in Ireland, there were settlements created in Dublin, Waterford, and Cork.

Sometime between 849-852 AD, there were new Vikings that arrived in Ireland and they were known as the Danes. Those who called Ireland home called these Vikings the dark foreigners. The Vikings that had been in Ireland for a while – the Norse- named the Danes the fair foreigners and it did not take long for both sets of Vikings to get into a war over the Strangford Lough and the Irish sea.

# Attacks on the towns of Ireland

The Vikings that were in Waterford attacked the Israige king in 860 AD. After this attack, the attacks against the Vikings increased. It wasn't until six years later that the longphort settlement was gotten rid of in one of these attacks and the King of Northern Ui Neill got rid of any Vikings that were in Ulster. It was then in 887 AD that the Vikings of Limerick were slaughtered by the men of Connacht. Then, the Vikings of Wexford, St. Mullins, and Waterford were slaughtered by 892 AD.

The ten years that followed forced the Vikings to move on and attack other places in Europe, however, they found that this was harder than attacking the towns in Ireland so they returned in 914 AD with more men than they had before. The

Vikings from Britain joined in on the attacks now by way of the Irish sea.

Sometime in 919 AD Niall Glundubh died and therefore the city of Ulster was open for attacks from the Vikings that were raiding the surrounding towns. But, in 924 AD, five years later, there were thirty-two ships that came into Lough Foyle and the Vikings returned to restart their settlements.

Thus, Ireland was the slave to the power of the Vikings and the numbers that they had. Thankfully, this was not going to last long.

## Irish monasteries

Because the monasteries that were in Ireland did not have any defenses, they were the primary target of the attacks from the Vikings both times that they inhabited Ireland. This caused round towers to be built so that they were more protected from the Vikings.

These round towers only had one entrance and it was about ten feet off the ground making it to where a ladder had to be used so that one could get into the tower. Today, these towers are still standing in Ireland and their unique features are still standing strong as well.

## The Irish rebel

Muircertach, the son of Niall Glundubh wanted to get revenge for the death of his father so he began to plan attacks from where he had set up base in Grianan Aileach.

All of the battles that Muircertach had against the Vikings ended up in a victory for him which caused him to move on to the Scottish Isles so that he could continue attacking the Vikings. However, in 943 AD, Muircertach died in battle.

When Munster got a new king, the king called himself the High King of All of Ireland once his brother was killed during battle. This king went on to continue the slaughter of the Vikings that were in Dublin and then in 1002, he was finally recognized as the high king indeed.

## No victory in sight

Due to the fact that the Vikings tried to get into the internal affairs of Ireland, they failed to take over the island. Therefore, the Vikings joined up with the clan that was in Leicester and went on to make plans defeat King Brian Boru. In order to do this, any and all Vikings were welcomed to come to Ireland to help.

In 1014 on Good Friday, there was a fleet of Vikings that landed in Dublin so that they could try and defeat Brian Boru. The army that Brian was fighting with was the Munster army along with some Vikings from Limerick and Waterford who had given up trying to take over the island and joined forces with the king.

While praying for victory during a battle, Brian was struck down at the age of seventy. After this, the Vikings were pushed back to their ships while losing a great many of their forces. This battle is what caused the Vikings to lose any power that they had in Ireland forever.

Just because the Vikings never took over Ireland does not mean that they went away. They continued to help Ireland advance in ways of technology such as building ships and weapons as well as learning new battle tactics. There were towns such as Dublin and Waterford that were built with the help of Vikings.

Some Vikings did leave the island, but not all of them did. Those that did not marry into the Irish families that were already settled there and became a part of the fabric that would shape Ireland for any future generations.

Because of the Vikings that invaded Ireland along with some internal disputes that were going around the island, the Church that was located in Ireland was reduced in power. This caused Rome to worry that Ireland was moving away from their Christian roots and it made them believe that Ireland needed to be reformed and disciplined.

In an effort to bring Ireland back to Christianity, Malachy of Armagh was appointed the Bishop of Down and Conner.

# Chapter Six: St. Patrick

St. Patrick is more than just a holiday where we celebrate being Irish and drink and have fun. In fact, St. Patrick was a real person and he had a huge impact on the history of Ireland as well as one of everyone's favorite holidays!

St. Patrick is known as a patron saint of Ireland is one of the most recognized figures in the Christian religion. Although he is widely celebrated, we do not actually know a lot about how he lived his life whenever he was alive. There are tons of stories that you can locate that are going to be associated with St. Patrick which include things such as him banishing snakes from Ireland, but sadly, most of these are nothing more than fairytales that have been made up by expert storytellers.

St. Patrick was born in Britain sometime around the fourth century to a set of wealthy parents. His death is rumored to have occurred sometime on March 17$^{th}$ in 460 AD.

Patrick's father was a Christian deacon but people believe that this role was taken because of all of the incentives that he got on his taxes due to the fact that there are no signs that point to the fact that Patrick's family was one of religion.

## Captured by the Irish

Whenever Patrick was sixteen, a group of Irish raiders attacked his families estate and took him, prisoner, sending Patrick to Ireland where he would be held in captivity for around six years. It is hard to say exactly where Patrick was held during this captivity, there are some people who believe that he was in Mount Slemish while others believe it was County Mayo.

Never the less, while Patrick was being held in captivity, he worked outdoors as a shepherd and was not allowed to be near people most likely for fear of him telling someone what had happened. It was during this time period when Patrick was alone and afraid of what his future held that Patrick finally turned to the religion in which he had known as a child which then lead him to become a devout Christian.

There is another rumor that states that Patrick actually dreams of converting people in Ireland to the Christian religion while he was being held in captivity, but there is no evidence of this that has been found.

## Visions

Sometime during his captivity Patrick finally managed to escape. In what has been found of St. Patrick's writing, he states that a voice told him that it was time for him to leave Ireland and that Patrick believed that it was God telling him this.

However, in order to escape, Patrick had to walk around two hundred miles from where he was being held to the coast. Once he made it to the coast, Patrick found his way back to Britain. After he had made it back to his homeland, another vision came to Patrick that to him that he needed to return to Ireland, but as a missionary this time.

It was after this vision that Patrick took up religion training for about fifteen years where he earned his ordination as a priest. Once he was ordained, Patrick now returned to Ireland with two things in mind. One was to minister to the Christians that were already residing in Ireland. The other was to try and convert the Irish that did not believe in Christianity. Strangely enough, what Patrick was sent to do is different than what many believe and that St. Patrick is actually the one who introduced Christianity to Ireland in the first place.

# Crosses and bonfires

Being that Patrick was already familiar with the culture and the language in Ireland, Patrick used this to his advantage and started to incorporate the rituals that the Irish did into the lessons that he taught on Christianity. This was his way of trying not to get rid of the beliefs of those who lived in Ireland completely.

One example of how he did this was that he had bonfires lit on Easter being that the Irish honored many of their gods with a fire. A sun was also placed onto the Christian cross so that it became a new kind of cross, one of which we know as the Celtic cross. This was done so that it seemed more natural for the Irish to be okay with such a Christian symbol thus making their worship and transition to Christianity as painless as possible.

This was not to say that there were not already Christians that lived in Ireland whenever Patrick first arrived as a priest, but a great majority of the island was more nature-based pagans.

Since the Irish culture is very rich on telling their myths and legends, it is easy to see how St. Patrick's life became grander than it actually was.

# Legends of St. Patrick

There are plenty of legends that surround Saint Patrick, and here are just a few of the ones that are passed down amongst those in Ireland.

# The shamrock

It is said that Saint Patrick taught the Irish about the Christian ideal of God, Jesus, and the Holy Ghost forming a holy trinity by using a shamrock as a way to show that God was three people in one God. You can first locate this story being told in 1726 although it is very possible that it is older than that. Ever since this story, the shamrock has been the single biggest icon of St. Patrick's Day.

Back in the days when Ireland was still primarily pagan, there were a lot of them that believed in triple deities which may have helped Patrick in trying to teach them the Christian views he had been sent to preach.

Researchers say that little to no evidence exists that the Pagans help the shamrock as some sort of spiritual object. But, another researcher states that it may have been used to represent the powers of nature that were regenerative and when Patrick used it to describe the holy trinity is, it became a Christian icon.

Many pictures show Patrick with a shamrock in one of his hands and a cross being held in his other. Roger Homan wrote:

"We can perhaps see St Patrick Drawing upon the visual concepts of the triskele when he uses the shamrock to explain the trinity."

# Banishing the snakes

Due to the fact that there are no snakes in Ireland, many people believe that Patrick banished them all from the island, casting them off into the waters after attacking him during one of his prolonged fasts. The inspiration behind this legend comes from the story of Moses that can be found in the Bible when Moses and his brother Aaron used their staffs to fight against the sorcerers that worked with Pharaoh their staffs morphing into snakes and consuming all the other snakes that were in the area.

But as is explained in a later section, there have never been any snakes in Ireland. As a result, there wasn't anything for Patrick to rid the island of, in the first place.

# Patricks' walking stick

A few of the legends that you find in Ireland involve the Copog Phadraig, the Caoranach, and the Oillipheist. While Patrick was spreading the word of God in Ireland, it is said that he carried a staff that was made of ash wood. This stick would be thrust into the ground when he was preaching.

Today, it is said that at Aspatria (Ash of Patrick) the message that he was preaching took so long that by the time he was done, his stick had grown roots and had begun to sprout into a tree.

# The ancient ancestors and Patrick speak

A work from the 1100s called *Acallam na Senorach* gives the reader the story of how Patrick met with two of Ireland's ancient warriors while he was on his mission to convert the pagans. It is unsure of how these two warriors survived to make it to the time that Patrick was there, nevertheless, Patrick took the time to try and convert the warriors to his religion all the while they defended their religion of paganism.

## Saint Patrick's Cross

Patrick has two crosses that are commonly associated with him. One is the cross pattee while the other is the saltire. The pattee is the cross that you will find associated with Patrick. The saltire can be dated back to 1783 and is often associated with the order of St. Patrick.

There is no real reason that can be found as to why the cross pattee is associated with Patrick. One theory is that the bishops are oftentimes shown associated with them. Patrick is one of the founding bishops of the Church in Ireland, so this is how this symbol may have become associated with Patrick. Many pictures that show St. Patrick show him with in a bishop's clothing, all of which decorated with the cross pattée.

Even today the cross pattee can be associated with Patrick because it appears on the arms of the Roman Catholic Archdiocese of Armagh along with the Church of Ireland Archdiocese of Armagh. This is often believed to be done because Patrick was the first diocese in Armagh. The Down District Council also uses it on their headquarters in Downpatrick which is considered to be the place where Patrick was buried.

The Saltire of Patrick is red on a white field and is normally used to represent the order of St. Patrick which was founded in 1783. The Acts of Union that happened in 1800 caused the Saltire to be combined with the Cross of England, the cross of Scotland, and thus the union flag was formed. This is the flag that is commonly associated with the United Kingdom of Great Britain and Ireland.

However, the saltire has no references to St. Patrick.

# Saint Patrick's Bell

In the national museum of Ireland sits a bell that is known as St Patrick's bell. The first mention of this bell dates all the way back to 552.

The bell is considered to be a relic that was removed from Patrick's tomb about sixty years after he died. The bell is said to be the Bell of the Testament which is one of the most precious relics that Ireland has.

# Places that are associated with St. Patrick

- Slemish, County Antrim as well as Killala Bay, County Mayo: whenever Patrick was captured, these are said to be one of the two places that he was held, however, no one is sure exactly which one is the truth.
- Saul, County Down: legends say that Patrick's first church was founded in a barn in Saul. This caused Patrick to become a local chieftain. Patrick supposedly died in Saul as well. There is a rather large crest of Patrick here as well.
- Hill of Slane, County Meath Muirchu moccu Machtheni: Patrick is said to have lit a fire as his way of defying King Laoire. The story goes on to stay that the fire was not able to be put out by anyone who was not Patrick. He also told his story about the holy trinity with the use of a shamrock.

- Croagh Patrick, County Mayo: Patrick is said to have climbed the mountain and sat for the forty days of Lent. It was here that Patrick was able to bring in thousands of pilgrims that made their way up to the top of the mountain on the last Sunday in July.
- Lough Derg, County Donegal: Patrick killed a large serpent in the lake here according to lore and the water turned red because of the blood from the snake. Every August there are people who spend up to three days fasting and praying next to this lake.
- Armagh, County Armagh: Patrick started a church here and made it to be the holiest church to be founded in Ireland. Today this is the primary place for the church of Ireland. Both of the cathedrals for these churches are in towns that were named after Patrick.
- Downpatrick: Patrick was claimed to have been brought to this town when he died so that he could be buried.

## Places named after Patrick

- Ardpatrick, County Limerick
- Patrick Water, Elderslie, Renfrewshire
- Patrickswell
- St. Patrick's Chapel, Heysham
- St. Patrick's Island, County Dublin
- Old Kilpatrick
- St. Patrick's Isle
- St. Patrick's Newfoundland and Labrador
- Llanbadrig
- Templepatrick
- St. Patrick's Hill, Liverpool
- Patreksfjorour, Iceland
- Parroquia San Patricio y Espiritu Santo Loiza, Puerto Rico

# St. Patrick's Day

Everyone knows about St. Patrick's Day. Going also by the name "the Feast of Saint Patrick", the day is known as a religious and cultural celebration that is traditionally held on the seventeenth of March when it is said that St. Patrick died.

It was not until the early seventeenth century that the Christians and Catholic's began to observe the holiday. It is considered to be the day that Christianity was brought over to Ireland by St. Patrick; it also celebrates the culture and heritage of the Irish.

Those who celebrate St. Patrick's day in a more religious manner as it was intended to be, it is they spend the day for spiritual renewal and prayers often offered up for the missionaries that are spreading the gospel worldwide.

# Fun facts

### Snakes in Ireland

This is a myth that came around about St. Patrick is that he drove all of the snakes out of Ireland. There are no snakes that actually live in Ireland because of the waters being too frigid around the island, therefore, it makes it to where it is too cold for any snake to actually live on the island. However, it is common that this may just be a metaphor for getting rid of the pagan ways of those who called Ireland home.

## Partying

Up until 1970, St. Patrick's Day did not involve a lot of partying. Instead, it was mainly focused on the religious aspects of the holiday. However, when the 70's came around, the restrictions on people eating meat, dancing, and drinking were lifted for the day.

When the Irish came to America, that was when the party started. It is uncertain when the first parade actually took place, but the earliest that we can trace back the celebrations is to Boston in 1737 as well as New York 1762. Each year that passed and more Irish immigrants came to the US.

Some of the major parties that everyone around the world knows about is the parade that happens in New York and Chicago always dying their river green in celebration.

## Green

Many people believe that if you do not wear green on St. Patrick's Day, you are going to get pinched. However, why is this? A lot of the connection to the color green comes from the fact that there is a lot of green in Ireland when spring comes around, plus there is green in the Irish flag. Oh, and let's not forget that the island of Ireland is known as the Emerald Isle. One more thing that brings about the wearing of green is the fact that if you do not wear green, then a leprechaun is going to see you and pinch you.

## Shamrocks

It is said that Patrick used a shamrock as a way to explain the holy trinity when he was spreading Christianity. But, the shamrocks did not become a thing until the seventeenth century.

## Leprechauns

Leprechauns are not real, but they do come from popular Irish folklore. These small people were the shoemakers who took what they made from making shoes and put them in a pot at the end of a rainbow. People often times look for leprechauns to try and get them to give away a piece of gold, but also because leprechauns are supposed to be good luck!

## Corned beef and cabbage

This is a meal that is traditionally served on St. Patrick's day. Corned beef was chosen because cows were not usually slaughtered for meat in Ireland but were used for milk as well as the strength they provided. But, once again, corned beef and cabbage came from America going back to the Irish immigrants that were living in New York. These immigrants were buying their meat from butchers that were kosher as to not let go of their roots.

The corned beef and cabbage are more of a Jewish tradition where the corned beef and cabbage is put into a pot with potatoes and carrots. In Ireland, the corned beef is typically lamb or bacon.

# Chapter Seven: The Irish Rebellion

The Irish rebellion is also known as the United Irishmen Rebellion. This rebellion took place in 1798. The whole reason behind the rebellion was an uprising against the rule of the British that was in Ireland. It was a republic revolutionary lead by the United Irishmen. It is believed that this rebellion was inspired by the revolutions that had happened in America and France.

## Background information

The Williamite war ended in 1691 and ever since, Ireland has been under the rule of the Anglican Protestant Ascendancy, which was founded by the Church of Ireland who was primarily loyal to Britain and the British crown. How this ascendancy governed was mostly through sectarianism which was codified inside a set of penal laws. These laws did not favor anyone who was Irish Catholic or not an Anglican protestant.

It was in the eighteenth century were the elements that were in place were there and inspired by the Revolutionary war that took place in America. And it was this that caused the Irish to want to rise up and fight against the catholic populace so that they could reform and be separated from Britain.

# Society of United Irishmen

Wanting reform is what inspired a group of Protestant liberals which brought about the Society of United Irishmen sometime in 1791. This group was made up of several different religious men that were considered to be those that were lower class than the Catholics and the Protestant Ascendancy.

This society wanted a more democratic reform and emancipation from the Catholics. The Irish parliament was not going to give this emancipation. Whenever the war broke out with France in 1793, King Louis XVI was executed and the United Irishmen were sent underground and were pushed towards an insurrection with the French helping them out.

The Society of United Irishmen were trying to break the connection that Ireland had with England and in an effort to get more people on board with this, the society tried to spread out throughout Ireland. Sometime around 1797, there were 200,000 members in the society ready to fight for their independence.

As they continued growing in numbers, the Society of United Irishmen got together with a group that was against the Catholics called the Defenders. In 1793, the groups began to get arms by raiding homes in Ireland.

Even though they had a large number of people, the United Irishmen were still trying to get help from the military that had helped in the revolutionary that happened with the French government.

In an effort to get intervention, Theobald Wolf Tone who was the leader of the United Irishmen would travel from the United States to France to meet with people and try and get the help that they needed.

## 1796

All of the work that Tone put in paid off and eventually there were 14,000 French troops that had gone to Ireland to aid in the rebellion. There was also a French fleet that was going to help out. However, because they had to evade the Royal Navy along with storms, poor seamanship, and the fact that the leaders could not make a decision, they would eventually be beaten out.

Being that the French fleet had to go home, the veteran army was split up and sent to fight in other theaters.

## Counterinsurgency and repression

There was an establishment that responded to the disorder that was occurring in Ireland by causing a counter campaign that resulted in martial law. This counter attack caused houses to be burned, people to be murdered, and captives to be tortured. Most of these attacks took place in Ulster being that this was where a great majority of Catholics and Protestants resided.

In 1797, the military that was in Belfast suppressed a newspaper by using violent methods. This newspaper was the paper for the United Irishmen known as the Northern Star.

The British establishment thought that sectarianism was a good tool that they could use against the United Irishmen, and also took well to using the divide and conquer method. It has been found that Brigadier General C.E. Knox wrote General Lake stating:

"I have arranged to increase the animosity between the Orangemen and the United Irishmen, or liberty men as they call themselves. Upon that animosity depends the safety of the center countries of the North."

It is also written by The Earl of Clare to the Privy Council sometime during June of the year 1798:

"In the North nothing will keep the rebels quiet but the conviction that where treason has broken out the rebellion is merely popish."

The hope of the Earl was that he would be able to make sure that the Presbyterian republicans would not rise should they think that the Catholics were supporting the current rebellion.

While the rebels had their support, there was also loyalist to the government that were supplying local intelligence and supplying recruits to the Orange order that came around in 1795. This was the same year that the Maynooth college was founded by the government. It did not matter what was happening, the Irish Church was going to support the British crown.

There was intelligence that was given to the government from informants that had gotten into the United Irish in 1798 that made the government take out most of the leaders that were residing in Dublin during the raids. Martial law continued to be imposed throughout the country and there was an unrelenting brutality that caused the United Irish to act before they no longer had the option.

# Rebellion

The plan was for Dublin to be taken over so that reinforcements could not get into the city. This plan was spread through the mail coaches that traveled around Dublin. But, because of the informants telling the government what was going to happen, there was barely enough time for the rebels to do what it was that they needed to do.

A great number of rebel leaders were then arrested causing the rest of the rebels that were gathering to disperse quickly abandoning their plan.

Despite the fact that their plan did not work, the districts that surrounded Dublin rose like they had planned to and pretty soon so did most of the counties. The very first clashes that signaled that the rebellion was taking place happened on the twenty-fourth of May.

It did not take long for the fighting to spread. A great majority of the fight happened in County Kildare. The army was able to beat off many of the attacks that the rebels made, however, the rebels were able to gain control of the country while the military withdrew.

It was in County Wicklow that the news about the rebellion caused panic and the loyalist decided that they were going to kill anyone who was in custody for being suspected of supporting the rebellion. Sir Edward Crosbie was found to be leading the rebellion that was taking place in Carlow and thus was executed on the order of treason.

# Aftermath

Not many, but some of the rebel armies survived for several years thanks to the use of guerrilla warfare. General Joseph Holt was one that fought with his comrades up until he was forced to surrender in 1798. Whenever Robert Emmet failed in 1803, the last of the rebels capitulated. However, there were still some rebels that managed to hang on until the following year.

In 1800 the Act of Union was passed but did not come into effect until January of the following year which took away any autonomy that had been granted to the Protestant Ascendancy that was located in Ireland.

The biggest reason this act passed was because of the rebellion that had just taken place which was provoked thanks to the misruling of the Ascendancy under British leadership.

# Chapter Eight: The Nine Years' War

Quite obviously the nine years war lasted for nine years. It was a war that was waged from 1594 to 1603 in Ireland. It is also known as Tyrone's Rebellion and was fought between the Gaelic Irish and the English that were ruling in Ireland at the time. No part of the country was left untouched by this war but, it was mostly fought in the province of Ulster. In the end, the Irish were defeated and exiled in the Flight of the Earls.

This war was against O'Neill and those that decided to side with him is considered to be one of the largest wars that were fought by England during the Elizabethan era. During the climax of the war, there were around 18,000 soldiers that were from England fighting in Ireland. This is compared to when the English fought alongside the Dutch in the Eighty Year's War where the numbers were never more than 12,000 at a time.

## Causes

The Nine Year's War was caused when a Gaelic Irish chieftain by the name of Hugh O'Neill decided to wage war against the English State that had taken over Ireland at the time. The only people that O'Neill was able to get to fight by his side were those who were not happy with how the English government and even the Catholics were not allowing Protestantism to spread throughout Ireland.

# The crown and Ulster

In the early times of 1590, the attention of Lord Deputy Fitzwilliam was drawn to north Ireland who was the one who was supposed to be bringing Ireland under the rule of the English crown.

During this time period, there was a provincial presidency that was proposed and Henry Bagenal was the one who ended up running for it and getting it thanks to the Dublin government. However, O'Neill had married Bagenal's system against her brother's wishes. This is where a bitter rivalry began and was made stronger whenever Mabel died just a few short years into her marriage due to the fact that O'Neill was neglecting her and paying attention to his mistresses.

When 1591 came around, the MacMahon lordship was broken up by Fitzwilliam whenever the leader of the sept resisted the English sheriff which caused him to be hung. Several more lords were forced into the same fate and even O'Neill was forced into it. However, he managed to resist thanks to his force of arms.

# War

Hugh O'Donnell had gotten rid of the English Sheriff in 1592 by driving him out of his territory. The next year O'Donnell paired with Maguire to resist the introduction of a new sheriff which caused attacks to begin at the English outposts along the edge of Ulster.

O'Neill assisted the English at first attempting to gain something for himself. Sadly the queen feared that O'Neill would not be a simple landlord and that he would try and take over so that he could become Prince. It was this very reason that caused O'Neill to join in the rebellion in 1595 by attacking the English fort that resided on the River Blackwater.

Later on that year, King Philip the second got a letter from O'Neill and O'Donnell with a proposal to be the Kings vessels along with his cousin being made the official prince of Ireland. January of the next year they got their reply from the king encouraging them to go on and do what it was they needed to get done. However, the armada sailed unsuccessfully which caused the war that was going on in Ireland to become a part of the Anglo-Spanish War that was currently going on.

## An Irish victory

The English that had the castle in Dublin were not quite aware of how large the rebellion actually was. When negotiations failed in 1596, the armies that were in Ireland for England tried to get into Ulster but were repelled by an army that was trained and included musketeers.

The English lost the Battle of Clontibret and were driven back in the years that followed. However, when the Battle of the Yellow Ford began in 1598, there were around two thousand English troops that were killed because they were ambushed as they made their way to Armagh. The troops that did make it, managed to get safe passage for themselves only by promising that they would evacuate the city.

Henry Bagenal, the personal enemy of O'Neill was killed during an earlier engagement which ended up being one of the heaviest defeats that the English army suffered up to that point.

Thanks to mercenaries helping out, there were victories all over the country that were in O'Neill's pay. It was at this point that the war had developed to what would be its full force. Some of O'Neill's biggest supporters were appointed as chieftains.

There were not many of the native lords that could continue to be loyal to the crown and those that had tried to remain loyal were forced to watch their kinsmen and even their followers turn and begin to support the rebels.

Despite all of the cities that had been fortified and sided with the English government, O'Neill could not take any of the cities that had been walled in even though he made repeated overtures of those that were living off the Pale so that they could join him. He used their religion and their alienation from the government in Dublin to try and get them to switch over.

Those that were old English were mostly able to remain hostile to the Gaelic enemies and stay loyal to the crown.

# The rebellion ends in Munster

Around the middle of 1601, the English Lord President over Munster had gotten the rebellion to quit in Muster by using force and conciliation. That summer, the main castles in Muster were taken back and the Irish had scattered.

All of this was accomplished by negotiating a pact with the main Gaelic Irish leader that was in the area which then allowed for MacCarthy to be neutral all while the English Lord President was allowed to keep focusing on attacking people like Fitzgerald. MacCarthy kept resisting the raiding parties that were occurring in his area, but he would not go to the aid of Fitzthomas despite the fact that O'Neill and O'Donnell were asking him to.

# End of the war

It was in 1602 that O'Neill finally destroyed the capital that was at Dungannon as the Mountjoys approached, and from there he went to hide in the woods. It was Mountjoy that destroyed the inauguration stone that was for the O'Neill's in Tullaghogue.

Not too long after that, famine came to Ulster and the earth was scorched to try and get it to produce again. All of those that served under O'Neill surrendered and O'Donnell eventually did too at the end of the year 1602.

O'Neill was able to hold out until 1603 because of how large the forest that he was hiding in was. At the time of his surrender, there was the signing of the Treaty of Mellifont.

March 24th of that year, Queen Elizabeth died.

# Chapter Nine: Bloody Sunday

Bloody Sunday is one of the most violent days in the history of Dublin and it occurred on the twenty-first of November in 1920 all during the War of Independence for Ireland. There were thirty-one people that were killed, eleven of them being British soldiers, three Irish Republic prisoners, and sixteen Irish civilians.

Michael Collins had organized the IRA (Irish Republican Army) and given them orders to kill the Cairo Gang which was a team of British intelligence agents that were undercover in Dublin. The members of the IRA went to where they knew these intelligence agents were living and killed fourteen different people. Along with the fourteen that died, Montgomery was wounded and ultimately died of his wounds. One RIC (Royal Irish Constabulary) officer died, nine British army officers died, two civilians were caught in the crossfire, and two members who were part of the Auxiliary division died as well. One man by the name of Leonard Wilde could not be accounted for.

It did not take long for those that were part of the Auxiliary division and the RIC to open fire at a football match that was taking place in Croke Park. Fourteen different civilians were killed in this counter attack and about sixty were wounded.

Three members of the IRA were supposed to be being held in the castle in Dublin and they were beaten and killed by those who were holding them captive because they were trying to escape. If they were actually trying to escape or not is unclear, that that is what their captors said was happening.

While not many people were casualties of Blood Sunday, the IRA considered it to be a victory since the British intelligence was severely harmed by the plan that Collin's had come up with. However, there was no damage done to the guerrillas in the area, but it did increase the support that the IRA got from those who were in Ireland as well as those who were not.

## Bloody Sunday morning

It was the morning of November twenty-first that the IRA began their mission. Many of those that died were killed in what was considered to be a middle-class area just south of the inner city of Dublin. That is all but two of the shootings that took place at the Gresham Hotel on what is now known as O'Connell street.

Where the IRA had their most success in carrying out their plan was at 28 Upper Pembroke street where the IRA got the upper hand on three intelligence officers. Two of which ended up dying right away and another that ended up dying later as a result of his wounds that he received that day. At 38 Upper Mount Street, yet another two officers were killed bringing the IRA total up to five.
It was at 22 Lower Mount Street that the IRA ran into some trouble. One intelligence officer was killed while the other managed to get away. The building that was being occupied was then surrounded the auxiliary division and the IRA was forced to fight their way out. At least one volunteer for the IRA was wounded and captured by the division while at least two people who belonged to the auxiliary were captured and killed.

The sixth intelligence officer was killed on Morehampton road but a civilian was also caught in the crossfire in what is assumed to have been a mistake. Yet another civilian was killed at the hotel.

Collins, the one behind the attacks was able to justify the deaths that had taken place that morning by saying:

"My on intention was the destruction of the undesirables who continued to make miserable the lives of ordinary decent citizens. I have proof enough to assure myself of the atrocities which this gang of spies and informers have committed. If I had a second motive it was no more than a feeling such as I would have for a dangerous reptile. By their destruction, the very air is made sweeter. For myself, my conscience is clear. There is no crime in detecting in wartime the spy and the informer. They have destroyed without trial. I have paid them back in their own coin."

## Bloody Sunday afternoon

There was a football game that was being played at Croke Park in Dublin. Even though people knew about the killings that had taken place, they were going to continue with life as if nothing had happened. There were somewhere around five thousand people that had congregated in Croke Park.

However, in the crowd, there were security forces for the British that were going to raid the match. These troops came in on one side while police and auxiliaries came in from the other end. They were told that they needed to surround the park and not allow anyone to exit while they searched for IRA in the crowd.

It is said that they were supposed to tell everyone what was going to happen and that no one was going to be shot if they cooperated. However, this is not what happened. Shots were fired the moment that the police got to the stadium.

One eyewitness states:

"It is the custom at this football ground for tickets to be sold outside the gates by recognized ticket sellers, who would probably present the appearance of pickets, and would naturally run inside at the approach of a dozen military lorries. No man exposes himself needlessly in Ireland when a military lorry passes by."

A reporter for the Freeman's Journal in Ireland wrote:
"The spectators were startled by a volley of shots fired from inside the turnstile entrances. Armed and uniformed men were seen entering the field, and immediately after the firing broke out scenes of the wildest confusion took place. The spectators made a rush for the far side of Croke park and shots were fired over their heads and into the crowd."

The commander of the police force stated that his men were excited and had gotten out of hand. By the time they had gotten back under control and stopped firing, there were a hundred and fourteen rounds that had been fired out of rifles while fifty rounds came from machine guns, and an unknown amount came from the revolvers that the police carried.

Those who had survived the shootout were searched and then let go and nothing was ever found.

Not wanting to look bad, they tried to cover up what had happened at the park by releasing a press release.

"A number of men came to Dublin on Sunday under the guise of asking to attend a football match between Tipperary and Dublin. But their real intention was to take part in the series of murderous outrages which took place in Dublin that morning.

Learning on Sunday that a number of these gunmen were present in Croke Park, the Crown forces went to raid the field. It was the original intention that an officer would go to the center of the field and speak from a megaphone, invite the assassins to come forward. But on their approach, armed pickets gave warning. Shots were fired to warn the wanted men, who caused a stampede and escaped in the confusion."

## Bloody Sunday night

Two IRA officers by the name of McKee and Clancy both of which were part of the plan for the killings that had taken place earlier that day were being held captive at the Dublin Castle, both men were killed. As to why they were killed is unsure. Some say that the guard's state they were trying to get away, while others say because there was no room in any of the cells to hold them.

## Misconceptions

- The shooting that took place at Croke Park is often blamed on the Auxiliaries, but in reality, the RIC did a majority of the shooting that took place.
- There is a film called Michael Collins that shows a car being driven into the football stadium, this, however, did not actually happen. The shots that came from this car were fired into the air rather than into the crowd.
- People believed that two of the footballers had been killed, but only one was killed while another was uninjured.
- It is said that there was a coin that was tossed in deciding if the officers were going to go on a killing spree in the park or loot Sackville street.

# Chapter Ten: The Partition of Ireland

May third of 1921, Ireland split into two different divisions. One was the republic of Ireland in southern Ireland and the other was Northern Ireland. When you look at Ireland today, there is still a Northern Ireland that is part of the United Kingdom. Southern Ireland is known as a sovereign state and is called the Republic of Ireland.

It was the act of 1920 that was meant to create two territories that could govern themselves but still be part of the United Kingdom. When the War of Independence ended along with the Anglo-Irish treaty being signed, the southern part of the island became a free state.

Whenever Ireland parted, it was an aspiration of the nationalist to try and reunite Ireland so that all of it was an independent state. The goal, however, conflicted with that of the unionists that were found in Northern Ireland.

An agreement was reached in the Belfast Agreement of 1998 between the Irish and British governments that the status of the island would not change unless a majority of those who lived there could come to an agreement.

The northern part of the island thought the government that was in the UK was able to keep to the constitutional position that that part of Ireland currently had and they thought it was best for them to stick to being part of the United Kingdom.

# Background

There was the thought of excluding the counties of Ulster from the Home Rule bills because they thought that Ulster should have its own government. There was a unionist MP by the name of Plunkett who supported the home rule bills at a later date but opposed it during the 1890s due to the danger that Ireland would be vulnerable to if the island was to split.

The British cabinet first considered exclusion in 1912 due to the fact that unionists in Ulster were against the third home rule bill. The UVF (Ulster Volunteer Force) brought in somewhere around three million rounds of ammunition and twenty-five thousand rifles because of the fear that the home rule bill being passed would result in a civil war in Ulster.

At the Buckingham Palace Conference, the main discussion was the issue of the island splitting apart and it was believed that the nine counties in Ulster would all be separated.

# Ireland act

The Ireland act occurred in 1920 but was not put into effect until the next year. This government act made it to where the parliaments could govern themselves in Northern Ireland as well as southern Ireland. This is where the island officially became parted. Governmental institutions and Parliament were set up in Northern Ireland once the twenty-six counties gave their allegiance to Eireann while supporting the effort that was being put in for the Irish War of Independence. This caused southern Ireland to be left defenseless.

# Anglo-Irish treaty

The War of Independence had brought on the Anglo-Irish treaty. This treaty was given the proper legal effect that it needed inside of the United Kingdom thanks to the Irish Free State Constitution Act of 1922. This act was ratified by Eireann in Ireland. This act also made it to where Ireland became a free state.

However, the treaty and the laws that were enforcing it did not include Northern Ireland due to the fact that they had opted out of being part of the Republic of Ireland so that they could continue to be part of the United Kingdom.

# Northern Ireland

Whenever the treaty went into motion, the northern parts of Ireland were part of the free state until they decided to opt out. And, opt out they did. It was in 1922 that Northern Ireland exercised their right to opt out but it did not come without some hesitation.

When Northern Ireland opted out, the following address was made to the King.

"Most gracious sovereign, We, your Majesty's most dutiful and loyal subjects, the Senators and Commons of Northern Ireland in Parliament assembled, having learnt of the passing of the Irish Free State Constitution Act, 1922, being the Act of Parliament for the ratification of the Articles of Agreement for a Treaty between Great Britain and Ireland, do, by this humble Address, pray your Majesty that the powers of the Parliament and Government of the Irish Free State shall no longer extend to the Northern Ireland."

The king did not receive this address until the next day and under Article 14 in the treaty that was made, Northern Ireland would continue to be under the rule of the United Kingdom.

The king responded to the address by saying:

"I have received the Address presented to me by both Houses of the Parliament of Northern Ireland in pursuance of Article 12 of the Articles of Agreement set forth in the Schedule to the Irish Free State (Agreement) Act, 1922, and of Section 5 of the Irish Free State Constitution Act, 1922, and I have caused my ministers and the Irish Free State Government to be so informed."

Much like anything, there were those who did not like the treaty and the fact that Northern Ireland was able to stay part of the United Kingdom. Many debates occurred between Ireland and Parliament, but Northern Ireland had made their decision and the king was going to let them continue with that decision. Even today there are those that do not agree with what had happened so many years ago, however, there was an agreement that was put into place in 1998 that ratified both parts of Ireland so that there could finally be peace.

The Northern Ireland peace process has been in progress since 1993.

# Chapter Eleven: The IRA (Irish Republican Army)

The IRA stands for The Irish Republican Army and they had made several movements in Ireland during the twenty and twenty-first centuries in an effort to bring republicanism to all of Ireland. The main belief of the IRA is that they want to have an island that is an independent republic while also believing that they can and should use political violence as a way to take back what is, in their eyes, rightfully theirs.

The term IRA first was used during the raids on Fenian where a great majority of British landmarks, forts, and towns were destroyed. The original Republican Army was first formed in 1917 by the volunteers that did not enlist in the British Army when World War I was going on. There are members of the Irish Citizen Army and several others that had refused to join as well.

During the War of Independence, this was the army that had been declared by Eireann sometime in 1919. There were some of the Irish natives that will say otherwise and state that the organizations that have been created in more recent years are the only true descendants of the first IRA, which is sometimes referred to as "Old IRA."

One former IRA member by the name of Behan says that one of the first things that was on the agenda for the IRA was the split of Ireland. This was actually the main topic of the IRA. The very first split came in 1921 whenever the Anglo-Irish treaty was signed and those that supported the treaty created the

National Army which was in the newly created Irish Free State. Those that did not agree with the treaty were the ones who fell under the name of the Irish Republican Army.

Whenever the Irish Civil War finally came to an end, the RIA had been around for about forty years, but in 1969, the IRA split into two different groups. One known as the Official IRA and the other known as the Provisional IRA.

The Provisional IRA would have yet another split into the Real IRA and the Continuity IRA where everyone in these groups is claiming that they are the true descendants of the IRA.

The IRA was in place between 1917 and 1922 and was recognized by the First Dail as an actual army for the Republic of Ireland in the spring of 21. This group then split into two different forces, one that was for the treaties that were being signed and these were known as the Government forces or as the Regulars. Then those who were against the treaties and they were known as Executive forces, the Republicans, and even the Irregulars.

Those who were in the IRA and against the treaties fought in the Irish Civil War but lost and this caused them to not recognize that there was a Free State or even a Northern Ireland. Both the Free State and Northern Ireland were said to have been the creations of Britain. For about forty years, the IRA existed in one way or another until they split in 69.

The OIRA (Official Irish Republican Army) was what was left once the IRA split up into the two different groups. The OIRA was mostly made up of Marxist and was not active in a military sense instead turning to the political side of things. The Offical Sinn Fein became known as the Worker's Party of Ireland.

The PIRA (Provisional Irish Republican Army) was made up of those that did not want to join the OIRA in 69. These are the people who dealt with the violence that was happening in Northern Ireland. They were highly against the Marxism that the OIRA embraced and pretty soon they became part of the left wing orientation in politics.

The PIRA broke up and one group that came from it was the CIRA (The Continuity Irish Republican Army) sometime in 1986. This split happened because the PIRA had ended the policy that they had in place on abstentionism which ultimately made it to where they recognized an authority in the Republic of Ireland.

The other group that was made up from the split was the RIRA (The Real Irish Republican Army) and all the members of the real IRA were against the peace process that was currently going on in Northern Ireland.

It was not until April of 2011 that those who were part of the PIRA had made the announcement that there was a resumption of the hostilities in Ireland and they had taken care of the mainstream IRA. Going on, they continued to say that they are going to keep operating under the name of the Irish Republican Army because they were the IRA. However, this group was not part of the real IRA, the ONH, or the Continuity IRA. They even went on to take responsibility for the attack that happened on constable Kerr and several other attacks that have been claimed by the other two groups previously.

# Chapter Twelve: Ireland Today

When you look at the economy in Ireland today you can see that it is more diverse than it ever has been before. Not just that, but it is more sophisticated and they have integrated themselves into the global economy. At the beginning of the 90s, the modern industrial economy had begun to transform Ireland giving the nation a substantial income. Even though they are still heavily relying on agriculture, they produce goods that are sophisticated and could even rival their international competition. The big economic boom that Ireland experienced in the 90s was known as the Celtic Tiger.

While the Catholic church once held power in Ireland found that its influence had moved on to more socio-political issues and the bishops that were in place were no longer the ones who were sought out when advice was needed on how to influence the republic or how to exercise their political rights. Most of modern day Ireland has detached from the church and this can be explained as a result of the fact that people began to show an extreme disinterest in the doctrine that the church was trying to impose on the younger generations. Not only that, but they began to question the morality of those that were supposed to be the representatives of the church.

There was a case that got a lot of media attention and it was the case of the Bishop of Galway Eamonn Casey. In 1992, Casey resigned without warning once it had come to light that he may have been having an affair with a woman from America and had also had a child with her. Even more, rumors began to float about priests abusing children and even engaging in pedophilia. This caused a lot of the public to question if there was any creditability in the church and how effect what they were preaching truly was.

Sometime in 2011, the church closed the embassy at the Vatican because of all of the rumors – whether they were true or not-.

## Irish flags

The most well-known flag of Ireland is the tricolored one which sports a green stripe, a white one, and an orange one. The green is for those that are roman catholic, the orange is for the protestants, and the white is the peace that was desired between the two religious groups dating back to the nineteenth century.

The tricolored was presented by Thomas Francis Meagher who wanted to show the peace between the two different religions and he hoped that under the same flag would bring the Catholics and protestants together in brotherhood. There were a few that thought that the flag would one day be the banner that flew over the nation.

This flag was used in 1916 Rising and it was accepted by all the nationalists as the national flag and thus became the flag for the Irish Republic and the Irish Free State. It was not until 1937 whenever the Constitution of Ireland was brought to the island that the tricolored flag became the official flag of the nation.

Even though the tricolored flag is the flag that is commonly known as the flag of Ireland, it is not the official flag of

Northern Ireland. The official flag of Northern Ireland is the union flag that you can find in the United Kingdome. Although, not everyone agrees with it being used for Northern Ireland. The banner of Ulster is used in unofficial manners for the regional flag of Northern Ireland.

Ever since Ireland separated, there has not been a flag that has been accepted throughout the entire Ireland. However, a solution was to give four different flags to four provinces so that they could feel accepted and popular.

Some of the flags that have been used are:

- The tricolored flag of Ireland.
- The Saint Patrick's flag which has the cross and saltire of St. Patrick. This flag was used as the union flag once the Act of Union was signed.
- A blue flag that sported a harp was used during the eighteenth century. This flag is the standard flag for the president of Ireland.
- A green flag with a harp came in the nineteenth century and it was also used as the flag of Leinster

The flag that sported Saint Patrick's Saltire was used to represent Ireland by being used for the IRFU (Irish Rugby Football Union) before any other flag was adopted by the four provinces. The GAA (Gaelic Athletic Association) uses the tricolored flag for the entire island.

# Chapter Thirteen: Interesting Facts about Ireland

- The commonly known holiday of Halloween actually came from a festival that was celebrated in Ireland known as Samhain.
- The White House was designed by an Irishman by the name of James Hoban.
- Saint Patrick was not born Irish, he was Roman.
- Muckanaghederdauhaulia is the longest name in Ireland
- Ireland is home to more mobile phones than it is to people.
- The lakes are not called lakes but rather loughs. which is pronounced like locks.
- The most commonly spoken language in Ireland is Gaelic and then Irish and lastly English.
- Polish speakers outnumber those that speak Gaelic by about eight times more.
- Whenever a child has reached their birthday, they are to be held upside down and have their head bumped on the floor ever so slightly until they have reached the age that the child is. This is said to be for good luck much like the spanking tradition.
- Ireland has the largest consumption per capita at 131.1 liters a year
- The Titanic was actually made in Ireland.
- The Tara mine that is located somewhere near Navan is one of the largest zinc mines that can be found in Europe. It is also known as the fifth largest mine in the world.
- Irishman William Edward Wilson was the very first

person to be able to measure the temperature of the sun and be accurate about it!
- Ever since the Bronze Age, Ireland has held its own Olympics and they are called the Tailteann Games
- The maternity ward at the Rotunda hospital is one of the longest operating maternity wards in the world. The hospital is located in Dublin.
- James Boycott, an Irish Captain, coined the term boycott
- Over nine hundred years ago the pub Sean's Bar was founded and it is considered to be the oldest pub in Ireland.
- Ireland is the only country that you are going to find in the EU where you cannot have an abortion.

# Conclusion

Thank for making it through to the end of *Ireland*, let's hope it was informative and able to provide you with all of the tools you need to achieve your goals whatever it may be.

The next step is to take the knowledge that you gained by reading this book and put it to use in any papers that you may have to write about Ireland, or just to simply enjoy the fact that you know more about Ireland!

If you are ever visiting Ireland, you are going to know more about the history than what an average traveler is going to know and that will aid you in knowing what locations you are going to want to go and what you want to see.

Finally, if you found this book useful in any way, a review on Amazon is always appreciated!

# Free Kindle Books

**Sign up to my newsletter for free Kindle books.**

By joining my newsletter you will be notified when my books are free on Amazon so you can download them and not have to pay!

You will also be notified when I release a new book and be able to buy it for a reduced price.

You will also get a free **Spartans and the Battle of Thermopylae** book delivered to your inbox (in **PDF** format) that can be read on your laptop, phone, or tablet.

Finally you will also receive free history articles delivered to your inbox once a week.

Simply click the link below to signup and receive your free book:
**https://nostramo.lpages.co/patrick-auerbach**

Printed in Poland
by Amazon Fulfillment
Poland Sp. z o.o., Wrocław